LA CALLAS

First published in the United States of America in 1999
by UNIVERSE PUBLISHING
A Division of Rizzoli International Publications, Inc.
300 Park Avenue South
New York, NY 10010

and

THE VENDOME PRESS

Copyright © 1998 Éditions Assouline
English translation copyright © 1998 Éditions Assouline

Translated from the French by Louise Guiney

Front cover photograph: Maria Callas in *La Traviata*, at Covent Garden, June 1958.
© Sygma. Segalini Collection

Back cover photograph: Maria Callas and Aristotle Onassis in Monte Carlo, 1961.
© All rights reserved

ISBN: 0-7893-0381-7

Printed and bound in Italy

Library of Congress Catalog Card Number:

99 00 01 02 / 10 9 8 7 6 5 4 3 2 1

UNIVERSE OF STARS

LA CALLAS

ANDRÉ TUBEUF

UNIVERSE / VENDOME

O ther icons have achieved stardom. But when fame is followed by a profound solitude, then the star may rise to a higher level, becoming myth. Apart from Garbo, who in our century has gained this rare and elevated status? Monroe, perhaps? Callas, certainly. Callas's final days were marked by the same degree of isolation. Garbo and Monroe, however, may have been destroyed by their images; but Callas was first devoured by art and then the woman was destroyed by the fires of celebrity.

When we think of her, we see bouquets hailing down on an exhausted and transfigured Traviata at La Scala in Milan; and flashbulbs exploding in the wake of a silenced diva swathed in chinchilla, or seated at Maxim's, or hidden behind her legendary dark glasses. Callas the idol and Callas the victim played both roles in public. When her life ended, in the heart of the Paris *La Traviata* called *popoloso deserto,* the woman who had once been envied more than any other in the world had no one left for company in that world but her maid Bianca. Callas was a lightning bolt that electrified our de-mystified century. It is still reeling from the shock. Let us examine the myth more closely.

t he first paradox is that the neglected spirit of purest bel canto should have been revived in Maria Callas, who was born Greek, without a single drop of Italian blood in her veins, and who received an American education. Her parents were recent immigrants to New York when she was born, on December 3, 1923. Her pharmacist father shortened the unpronounceable family name Kalogeropoulos to Callas; her mother mourned a lost son and sought to avenge herself on life through her daughters. Jackie, the eldest by four years, was pretty and outgoing. Maria was the ugly duckling. She spoke with a Bronx accent, wore thick glasses to hide (or perhaps draw attention to?) her myopia, and stuffed herself with sweets. But she was gifted vocally. This was the period when Deanna Durbin was earning a fortune in Hollywood with her adolescent crooning, and Maria was thrust onstage by her mother, who entered her in radio talent shows. In 1937 the three women abandoned the pharmacist—a lackluster father and little-loved husband—and returned to Greece, where they resumed the name Kalogeropoulos. By this time, thirteen-year-old Maria's figure was so substantial, she could easily pass for at least sixteen. But her talent was substantial as well, and she was admitted to the conservatory. There she put her nose to the grindstone, signed up for extra classes, and was always the first to arrive and the last to leave. She wanted something more than gobbling candy. She envied others for the gifts she'd never possessed herself, and set out to acquire them through determination and hard work. She was still ridiculously young when she made her first stage appearances—performing in *Cavalleria Rusticana* at fifteen and *Tosca* at the tender age of nineteen. It was wartime; Athens was isolated, young talent was encouraged. The youthful Callas quietly watched, waited, and learned—slowly but surely.

Her real debut came five years later at Verona, in the summer of 1947. The Verona arena, built for Roman circuses, is a vast space requiring strong vocal projection. Playing La Gioconda, Callas gave it everything she had: a full-bodied, vibrant, bold, essentially physical sound. This was the perfect inauguration for a distinguished career in Italy, where she sang robust roles appropriate to an equally robust figure habitually stuffed into unflattering tweeds. She played Turandot, Aida, and even Wagner's Isolde and Brünnhilde. But there was still no hint of the metamorphosis to come. As a rule, fat opera singers simply grow fatter and more breathless with time, their girth denying them that "light-footedness" Nietzsche saw as the one true sign of grace in art. Callas herself never dreamt that one day she would become La Callas.

I n 1949 Maria Callas married Battista Meneghini, a Verona contractor old enough to be her father. Their meeting was far from romantic—he invited her to dine with him at a festival. But, although he tended to fall asleep over his newspaper at rehearsals, he showered her with all the things she had never had before: furs, a villa with fine carpets and paintings (by Veronese, of course)— all the opulence of success. She dressed in floral prints and wore a huge emerald that even von Karajan couldn't tear his eyes away from during rehearsals. Meneghini took over her business affairs, negotiating contracts shrewdly and aggressively, and keeping a sharp eye on the small print. Callas's genius began to shed the sparkle of a diamond in the rough. Her performance in *Traviata* at Parma was so alive, so genuine, that when Elisabeth Schwarzkopf heard it she immediately decided to give up the role herself. Maria Meneghini-Callas was now ready to conquer the world, but refused to appear in the United States—where she had been humiliated as a child—until she could do so on her own terms, triumphantly. First she built a reputation in Latin America, at the Teatro Colón in Buenos Aires and the Palacio de las Bellas Artes in Mexico City. Her Turandot and Aida were thrilling and unique; her high C and E-flat solid gold. Opulent in voice and body, she had carved out a path for herself.

We now leap over the quarter century that brought Callas worldwide fame, and pick up the thread again in Korea, at the ends of the earth and the end of the line. She's incredibly elegant and incredibly slender—not to say scrawny (and so is her voice, but haute-couture designers don't care about that), leaning on the arm of a tenor past his prime, accompanied only by a piano. Can this wan figure drowning in a sea of onlookers under glaring lights really be the same Callas? Her fire is now an ember, and will soon turn to ashes. For years she's been announcing a comeback, like an alcoholic promising to reform. Crowds throng to hear her, of course. Who wouldn't pay to see Lola Montez swaying on top of her ladder? On the eve of her 51st birthday, Callas suddenly has a fit of panic and cancels the tour. Last stop: Sapporo. Last stop but one, Hiroshima, where the memory of ashes on a cosmic scale should at least have inspired some twentieth-century Musset to compose a verse or two in honor of this shattered, latter-day Malibran, determined to survive. Eight years have gone by since she last sang in public. Pasolini's 1969 film *Medea* and the notorious New York Master Classes served merely as markers along a path of steady decline. In any case, neither at Portland in the spring of 1974, nor Fukuoka in the fall, could any member of the audience possibly have remembered or even imagined the former glory of this sorceress who, during a few brief seasons at La Scala with De Sabata, von Karajan, Bernstein, or Giulini in the orchestra pit, and Visconti directing, endowed the status of diva with new substance, and reinstilled into opera—commonly perceived as moribund—nobility, truth, and even popularity. Nevertheless, it is obvious that crowds such as these would never have turned out for an ordinary has-been.

What drew them? Certainly not her voice, although it was her voice that twenty years earlier had first made her a star. In Fukuoka, in Paris, in New York, no one cared about the artistic miracle Callas had once been. They came to gape at the heroine of a success-story in which an avid public scented—and vaguely hoped for—the spectacle of self-immolation. This is because, even as Callas was being devoured by her art, she was also rising to the second level of celebrity stardom; a level on which public response reflects criteria having little to do with false notes, and everything to do with false steps in love and behavior, and the prurient fascination they arouse. This renewal of fame on another level was historically unprecedented. Callas cannot be faulted for having sung her heart out in nineteenth-century operas; but she did turn her private life into an all-new international super-production—a media soap opera.

This is the key to understanding how her "re-cycled" magic brought such devastating solitude to Callas: the life of a singer who could sing no more culminated in unprecedented international celebrity. She lived out a destiny in which these two types of fame followed so fast upon each other that the second seemed almost a logical extension of the first. In her generation, Callas, and only Callas, had been prepared for operatic stardom of the first type. As a singer she brought audiences to their knees, but how many people actually made up those audiences of connoisseurs? Only a happy few, houses of two thousand multiplied by perhaps thirty-five performances in a good season, and many members of those audiences were the same people coming back for more. Meanwhile, her vocation—her vocal prowess!—was discovered by the recording industry which, having just come of age, provided her with the means not only to multiply her audience by thousands, but also to immortalize the magic of a single performance for all time. If genius is ten percent inspiration and ninety percent perspiration, then Callas amply qualified as a genius. She had done her homework, she was prepared. "Readiness is all," wrote Shakespeare, and she was ready. Suddenly, all those years of patient waiting and learning bore fruit. Furthermore, behind her first taste of international fame stood Walter Legge, artistic director for all the recordings she made during the decade of the 1950s. Legge did for Callas singing Italian opera what he had done for Elisabeth Schwarzkopf singing Mozart and Strauss, discerning in her a phonogenic quality that was not apparent on stage, but to which the microphone gave shades of unique truth and beauty. An artist who projects this phonogenic quality can turn recordings into invisible, endless, infinite theater. This is the asset Callas developed between the ages of thirty and thirty-five, and this is what made her the priceless, incomparable, unique diva she was, and set her apart from all those who had gone before her—of whom there were plenty, God knows!

A similar situation accounted for her elevation to the second level of fame. Through a fatal conjunction of circumstances ("readiness is all. . . "), the fledgling medium of photo-journalism was also coming of age. The first paparazzi serving the tabloid press and early television were as avid as they were novel, and Callas courted them. She led them on. They scented the blood of the tigress behind the singer, and they preferred the tigress, especially when she unsheathed her claws and (for example) threw a process server out of her dressing room during a contract dispute. Before she had sung a single note at the Metropolitan Opera, her run-ins with artistic director Rudolph Bing were already making headlines. She canceled a *Sonnambula* performance (for which she was not under contract), and spent the evening kicking up her heels at a party thrown by café-society hostess Elsa Maxwell. General consternation was raised to fever pitch in early 1958 when she stalked out of a *Norma* performance in Rome after the first act, leaving behind a glittering audience that included the president of Italy.

Callas had aroused the public's curiosity, but it is important to note a basic distinction. She was worshipped, she was adored; but she was not loved. An extensive cultural background was needed in order to appreciate her art: an art that was emotionally disturbing, an art that aroused passion, not pleasure. She was notorious for her harsh upper register. "Do you like my voice?" she once asked a fan for whom she was autographing a *Lucia di Lammermoor* album, "How can you?" Callas's singing demanded total, undeviating attention and a willingness to take risks. She wanted people to be swept away, to surrender. But she did not ask them to love her. Her rival Renata Tebaldi—she of the golden, honeyed voice—was infinitely less admired and never the subject of gossip; but she was easy to love, and people adored her.

The cameras were primed. Callas's "gala" performances were more spectacular than operas at La Scala, and they created the new, "media-event" performer. The perfect backdrop for one such event was the Paris Opéra, which had fallen upon hard times. Brigitte Bardot was in the audience, the Marquis de Cuevas interrupted an aria from *The Barber of Seville* to shout "Bravo!," and the master-of-ceremonies expatiated on how much weight the diva had lost. Having begun 1958 by causing a scandal before one European president, Callas ended it in triumph before another. Just when she was beginning to curtail her performances, she found herself in greater demand and more enthusiastically applauded than ever before. The figures are eloquent. In 1957, she gave thirty performances (including the historic premiere at La Scala) and recorded four complete operas. In 1958 she appeared thirty-two times, but did not perform a single complete opera. In 1959 she made only nine public appearances. Her dramatic presence, honed by working on stage under Visconti and enhanced by sublime clothes (on stage and off), became an opera in itself. But her voice was already faltering when, in the summer of 1959, on the arm of Meneghini—with whom she was celebrating her tenth wedding anniversary—she boarded the yacht *Christina* for a cruise with fellow-passengers Winston Churchill and (briefly) Greta Garbo. When she disembarked at the end of the cruise, she was on the arm of Aristotle Onassis.

Callas was, and remained, the leading star of the international opera circuit and arguably the most flamboyant, most sought-after, woman in the world. Theaters everywhere vied in their attempts to build her a bridge of gold. And yet, during the next six years she appeared a mere forty times on stage, primarily in London and Paris, for near-disastrous performances of *Medea* and *Norma* and, as often as possible, in the easier role of

Tosca in which simply to appear was almost enough. Here she was, the woman who at the height of her powers, on the La Scala stage, had been pelted with radishes as well as bouquets—radishes she graciously threw back at the audience or onto the edge of the stage, pleading myopia as an excuse—now, as those powers declined, receiving standing ovations and adulation, *prima donna assoluta* of the media hounds who track celebrities, create celebrities, but care next to nothing about grand opera. She transformed opera from a fashionable pastime into an obsession, and those who knew her only when she began to fail formed a cult of fanatics. Had Callas the meticulous and demanding perfectionist done all that work, in her heyday, in order to end up bending the ears of these would-be aesthetes? What a cruel joke of fate! Her self-destructive final performances as Norma enhanced her image as a tragic figure, but they did not improve her voice.

C allas moved from one level of stardom to the next so seamlessly, the second appeared to be an extension of the first. But, in fact, it inaugurated and gave credibility to another set of values, values against which, alone, against the tide of fashion and even in defiance of it, she had fought like a lion. This fighter was the true Callas, the great Callas, Callas-the-professional, as Nijinsky and Chanel were professionals. Fate played its joke with a heavy hand. The singer had first sacrificed the woman; and then the woman, grasping at an illusion of happiness, sacrificed the singer. There remained only the husk of a being who had never been able to find fulfillment or a shred of self-esteem through anything but her voice. As Oscar Wilde so aptly put it in his *Ballad of Reading Gaol:* "He who has lived more than one life must also die more than one death. . . ." A perfect description of this artist's fate.

Callas's exemplary rise was marked throughout by the practice of a single virtue, the most unforgiving of all: integrity. From a vast inferiority complex she drew the promise of triumph through perfectionism. Was she near-sighted? Then she must turn this flaw into a strength, and memorize all her scores, like Toscanini. When other people work to the letter they tend to become pedantic, but Callas transmuted the letter into spirit. Here lies the performer's sole genuine source of inspiration. Her vocal colors were intuitive, and hers alone—here an oboe, there a viola—learned from the modern, Wagnerian, orchestra, bringing to bel-canto technique a palette and a musical ear unlike that possessed by any of her predecessors. Her equally magical phrasing was sometimes out of step with the orchestra. "Look at me, Callas!" roared De Sabata (the same man who once said, "You can have no idea how fine a musician she is"). "You should look at me, Maestro," she replied sweetly, "you have better eyes than I do."

Her rule was always to do more than her share: the chorus is rehearsing *Alceste*, her call is for six o'clock but she arrives at three in order to get a feel for the sound that will greet her stage entrance. She comes to rehearsals in costume, so she can familiarize herself with *Traviata*'s forty pounds of paste jewelry or Iphigénie's eighteen-foot train. Visconti was stunned by the freedom of movement she acquired through this discipline. "She ran across a footbridge through a storm in her Iphigénie costume, sprang down the steps and stopped dead at the bottom, attacking her recitativo bang on the right note and the right beat." At Epidaurus she asked for the *Medea* staging created for tragedienne Katina Paxinou. Adjusting the demands of opera to a theatrical production was something she had mastered. In *Il Pirata*, when she was having trouble keeping up with the tempo, the conductor offered to slow it down for her. "Please don't," she replied, "I'm the one who must adapt."

In 1954 she set herself the goal of losing sixty-five pounds in ten months, but she lost them gradually, so as not to strain the muscles on which her breath control depended. When she next appeared, for rehearsals of *La Vestale* directed by Visconti, she was transformed: her hair in a neat chignon, her costume a chic little suit, her jewelry discreet pearls. Her gestures were serene and noble, reflecting the inner harmony she had finally achieved, one that was to be hers alone. Suddenly, her Italian became refined and polished, her English flawless. This all came about because, during work on *Medea* the previous year, she had conceived a hatred for her chubby figure and awkward movements. But a Maria Callas doesn't simply whip out a pencil and sketch a new self. She works from within, molding and mastering the face's bone structure until it projects the persona of the Ancients, until it becomes a theatrical mask and sounding-board, a projector for the voice. Callas turned herself into a musical instrument and a total performer. She donned the tunic of Nessus, wearing it next to her skin. And how she burned!

Callas had four or five fabulous seasons. She performed under Visconti's direction at La Scala as, successively, La Vestale—wearing pleated gowns that might have been designed by Grès; as La Sonnambula, for which she added graceful dancing to her vocal prowess; as Iphigénie, who, according to Gluck's fantasy, could infuse marble with life; and above all, as La Traviata, wearing black or blood-red gowns designed by Lila de Nobili in which she pursued her artistic destiny with smoldering ecstasy. At this point Callas had already been staking her life in a double-or-nothing game à la Lola Montez for seven years, ever since maestro Serafin, who masterminded her Verona debut, had thrust an unprecedented challenge upon her: sandwiched between the Venice performances of *Die Walküre* in January 1949, he had her try *I Puritani*, intermingling Bellini's hallucinatory score with Wagner's steely "Ho-yo-to-hos." The woman who—miraculously— was capable of meeting the greater challenge, also met the lesser one. Traditional bel-canto heroines were left behind her in their posturing roles as a gaggle of chirpy blondes or gesticulating bull-fighters' molls. With her boundless energy and Wagner-trained ear, and also with a virtuoso lightness of touch all her own, Callas became the only artist of her time finally able to don the legendary mantle of a Malibran or Pasta, daughters of fire who burnt to a cinder on stage and vanished at midnight. But she was not just dusting off museum pieces; she made Lucia, Elvira, and Amina the ardent sleepwalker contemporary, modern. The roles of Norma and Medea sucked her dry, and they were worth it. Callas bled herself white for them. But what other roles deserve self-sacrifice on this scale? By 1957 Callas had gutted the entire repertoire. All that remained were Anna Bolena and Paolina in *Poliuto*, which have great moments, but not the same overall impact.

Like all single-minded people, Callas was basically a simplifier. She never stopped to ask trivial questions, and either gave her all—or nothing. When she undertook the part of Anna Bolena, for example, she didn't pretend to have studied Tudor history, as others might have. She simply asked herself, "Who is she?" answering, "A queen." Her preparation for the role consisted in thinking like a queen, moving like a queen, becoming a queen. All or nothing, all the way. As she leapt to her death on stage night after night—at a time when performance was becoming more difficult for her—the temptation to do nothing must have been great. At last! Nothing!

No more death scenes on stage. Time to live a little.

Meanwhile, a Greek shipping magnate was searching for more fields to conquer. And thus did Aristotle Onassis come to play Jason the Argonaut to Callas's Medea. Their world was also a world of myth. Until the day when a chastened, vanquished, and exhausted Callas saw her contract as big-game hunter's trophy canceled. Onassis cast her aside, without ever having taken the trouble to marry her, so he could go after even bigger game, a woman seemingly widowed for all eternity by the blood of an assassinated president: an unattainable prize. Ah, but Onassis was monarch of a universe that revered the twin golden fleeces of power and fame. At Maria Callas's feet he had laid everything denied her by an impoverished childhood—and more besides: the merciless and grasping art of hedonism. Did he bear sole responsibility for turning her head? Alas, no. All too well aware that her days as an artist were numbered, Callas drained the proffered cup and willingly surrendered to this new bonfire of the vanities. She had worked so hard, given so much. Didn't she deserve a little happiness? She may even have thought this episode was transient, an extended holiday. What a relief to shed her fiery tunic, to be magically transformed from sorceress into Cinderella, to don the diaphanous gown of a fairy tale! The love story of these two parvenus who rose from nothing and arrived where everyone dreams of going was dazzling and incendiary. For the insatiable tycoon, it was just one more step on the ladder. But for the artist severed from the ascetic discipline that had made her what she was, it rang down the final curtain. Instead of leaping to her death on stage, she dined at Maxim's and cruised exotic isles. The spectacular soap opera written by Ari and Maria didn't need music, and it almost deprived us forever of Callas-the-singer. But she has survived, eternal and unique, in her recordings—that dark mirror into which she continued to peer when she was more dead than alive, a reclusive Castiglione who never realized she had become

16

a touchstone for all time.

Today Callas continues to cast her spell. On her records she lives again: whole, absolute, utterly demanding; opening our ears, teaching the truth every time someone who didn't know her when she was alive—who doesn't care which dresses Yves Saint Laurent designed for her, what her poodle was called, or the fee she extracted from Sapporo—discovers her recorded voice. Callas has survived her legend and reconquered her own truth. Sublime revenge. Today, in the theaters where she reigned supreme, theaters she transformed into holy temples, vain imposture is again the rule: gestures unconnected with the music, singing without style or schooling, all the things we thought her meteoric rise had brought to an end. But Callas also brought her own distinctive brand of theater to an end. She bore us to another land, initiated us into arcane secrets. Not to the land where a woman became an artist and the artist a role, even when the role was Norma, even if Norma was played with genius. What did Callas care about her own metamorphosis? As with any truly creative artist, she cared only about our metamorphosis. And, although superficially just a performer assuming a fictitious identity, a role, Callas was indeed truly creative, and she paid for the difference with her life. We are the ones she sought to transform, and we are the ones she succeeded in transforming, by using her discipline and intensity to make us listen in a new way. She gave eyes to our ears. We think we are simply listening to one of her records when, suddenly, we become spectators, our attention riveted by an artist of genius, the creator of all her metamorphoses: an artist who, working only with the audible, made herself visible and made us see. She accomplished this revelation without understanding it, but not without seeking it. She burned herself out in the attempt, and her fire still sheds light on us today. Here lies the magnificent mystery that was La Callas.

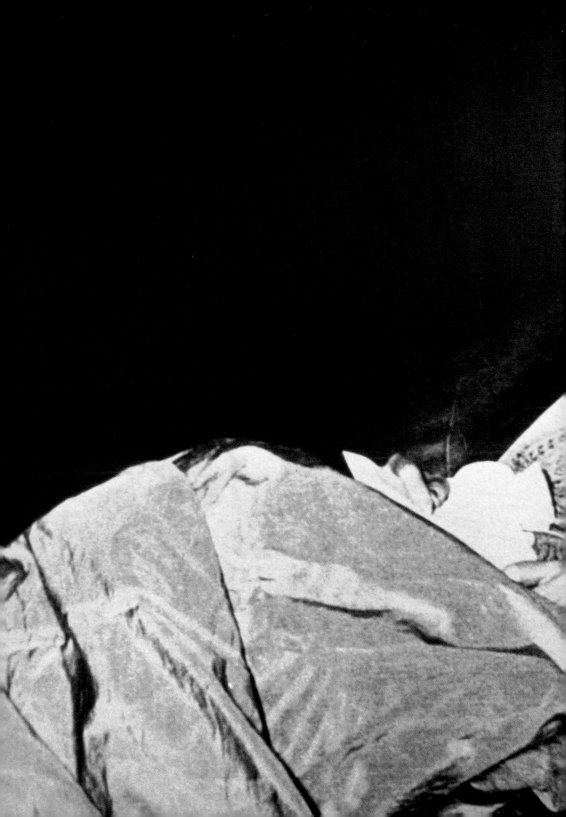

Chronology

1923: Maria Anna Sophie Cecilia Kalogeropoulos is born in New York, on December 3. Her parents, George and Evangelia, had emigrated from Greece to Long Island in August of the same year.

1929: George Kalogeropoulos changes the family name to Callas, and opens a pharmacy in the Greek section of Manhattan.

1932: Maria takes her first piano lessons. She was later able to practice all her roles alone at the piano, without the help of a vocal coach.

1937: Maria's parents separate. In March Evangelia returns to Greece with her two daughters, Maria and Jackie, and resumes the family name Kalogeropoulos. Although Maria is three years younger than the official age limit, she is accepted by the Athens Conservatory. She leaves school to enroll in the Conservatory, where she forms an important relationship with Elvira Hidalgo, her vocal teacher, and makes her debut at the Athens Opera. This pivotal year in Maria's career is also marked by her first amorous attachments, rivalries at the Athens Opera, and the onset of the Second World War.

1938: In November Maria obtains her first major operatic role at the Olympia Theater in Athens singing Santuzza in *Cavalleria Rusticana*, and wins the Conservatory Prize.

1942: *Tosca*, in Athens (July).

1944: *Fidelio*, at the Herod Atticus Theater in Athens (September).
Maria decides to return to her father in the U.S., and to resume the name Callas.

1947: *La Gioconda*, at the Verona Arena (August).

1948: *Turandot*, in Venice (January) and Rome (July).

1949: On April 10, Maria Callas marries Battista Meneghini, a wealthy Veronese contractor and opera fan.
Die Walküre and *I Puritani*, conducted by Tullio Serafin, at La Fenice in Venice (January). These performances mark a turning-point in her career, and launch her as an original interpreter of the Italian bel-canto repertory.
Callas makes her Latin American debut at the Teatro Colón in Buenos Aires with *Turandot*, *Norma*, and *Aida* (May-July).

1951: Callas tours Mexico City, São Paulo, and Rio de Janeiro with *Aida*, *Norma*, *Tosca*, and *La Traviata* (July-September).
Maria Callas opens the La Scala season in *I Vespri Siciliani* (December). For the next seven years, La Scala was to be the scene of her greatest triumphs.

1952: *Armida*, in Florence (April).
Callas makes her London debut in *Norma* (November), and then performs *Macbeth*, conducted by Victor De Sabata, at La Scala (December).
Callas begins a two-year weight-loss program, during which she sheds 65 pounds.

Sir Malcolm Sargent rehearsing Callas for a performance at Covent Garden, May 1961. © Archive Photos.

1953: In Florence, Callas records *Lucia di Lammermoor* (February) and *Tosca* (August), conducted by Victor De Sabata for EMI.

1954: *Lucia*, conducted by Karajan, at La Scala (January).
Debut in the U.S., at Chicago, with *Norma* (November).
A new, slimmer, Callas opens the La Scala season with *La Vestale*, conducted by Corelli and directed by Visconti (December).

1955: *La Sonnambula*, conducted by Bernstein and directed by Visconti, at La Scala (March).
La Traviata, with Giuseppe Di Stefano, conducted by Giulini and directed by Visconti, at La Scala (May).

1956: *Lucia*, directed by Karajan, in Vienna (June).
Debut at New York's Metropolitan Opera, in *Norma* (October).

1957: *Iphigénie*, directed by Visconti, at La Scala (June).
Café-society hostess Elsa Maxwell introduces the Meneghinis to Greek shipping magnate Aristotle Onassis at her costume ball in Venice.

1958: In Rome, Callas walks off the stage during the first act of *Norma*, at a performance attended by the president of Italy (January 2). Her high-handed attitude is severely criticized by the media.
In May, during the La Scala performances of *Il Pirata*, she locks horns with Antonio Ghiringhelli, managing director of the theater, and decides not to perform again at La Scala as long as he remains there.
She makes her debut at the Dallas Civic Opera, in *La Traviata*, and *Medea* (October-November).
Gala performance at the Paris Opéra, before an audience including the president of France.

1959: In July, Maria and her husband are invited by Aristotle Onassis for a cruise on his yacht, the *Christina*. At the end of the cruise, Maria leaves Battista Meneghini for Onassis. This liaison made Callas and Onassis the most publicized couple of the 1960s.

1960: *Norma*, at Epidaurus (August).

1965: Maria Callas is scheduled to give five performances of *Norma* in Paris (May). She doesn't feel well but decides not to cancel. On May 29, she ends the first scene of Act II in a highly weakened condition, and the last scene is canceled.
The final performance of Callas's operatic career is in *Tosca* at Covent Garden (July 5).

1968: Although Maria Callas believes Aristotle Onassis intends to marry her, he breaks off their relationship in order to marry Jacqueline Kennedy.

1969: Film version of *Medea*, directed by Pasolini (June-July). The film is a box-office failure.

1974: Final concert performance, with Giuseppe Di Stefano, in Sapporo, Japan (November 11).

1977: Maria Callas dies in Paris on September 17.

La Callas

The Callas family (originally Kalogeropoulos), soon after their arrival from
Greece. Left to right: Evangelia, Maria, Jackie, George. New York, 1924.
© Sygma. Segalini Collection.

The operatic mask and hand gestures of the youthful Signora Meneghini: a rare
and unique "raw material" destined to transform her into "La Callas."
© All rights reserved.
Callas plays Kundry the sorceress in *Parsifal,* Rome, 1949.
© Bianchi Ambroglio Collection. Photo: André Tubeuf.

The new Callas showing off every angle of her profile as Lucia, at Bergamo,
October 1954. © Sygma. Segalini Collection.

The best adulation of all: the chorus of *La Vestale* on-stage at La Scala, 1954.
Callas has brought to their knees both her director, Visconti (facing Maria,
demonstrating the gesture he wants her to make), and her co-star, Corelli.
© Archivio Fotografico Teatro alla Scala. Photo: Erio Piccagliani.

Callas's face in repose. Does being a diva mean being alone?
© Sygma. Photo: D. Goldberg.
La Vestale, **directed by Visconti,** La Scala, 1954.
© Archivio Fotografico Teatro alla Scala. Photo: Erio Piccagliani.

The sets for *La Traviata,* directed by Visconti: the scenes of Callas's self-
immolation. La Scala, 1955. © Archivio Fotografico Teatro alla Scala. Photo:
Erio Piccagliani.

Maria Callas in *La Vestale,* La Scala, 1954. The face, and genius, of the operatic tragedienne suddenly laid bare: a mask prepared to sing.
© Archivio Fotografico Teatro alla Scala. Photo: Erio Piccagliani.

La Callas during a recording session for *La Gioconda,* September, 1943.
© Sygma. Segalini Collection.
A foretaste of Medea. Maria Meneghini-Callas at the time of her debut in the U.S. Before the diva had achieved mythical status, a (very public) image of the tigress throwing out a process server sent to demand payment in connection with a contract dispute. Chicago, 1955. © Associated Press.

White robe, black robe. A haunting figure in *La Vestale,* directed by Visconti at La Scala in December 1954 (left); and an eerie one in *Medea* at the Royal Opera in London, 1959 (right). Left: © Sygma. Right: © Archive Photos.

Maria Callas in *Madame Butterfly,* which she only performed once on-stage (Chicago, 1955), before recording it under the baton of Herbert von Karajan.
© Sygma. Segalini Collection.
Callas played Turandot on-stage in 1947. Here she poses for the cover of the recording, made ten years later. © Sygma. Segalini Collection.

Profile and hand gestures. Callas as still life, at the height of her artistic mastery.
© Archivio Fotografico Teatro alla Scala. Photo: Erio Piccagliani.
Maria Callas and Giuseppe Di Stefano in *La Traviata.* The joy of a legendary duo bowing to their ecstatic audience. © Archivio Fotografico Teatro alla Scala. Photo: Erio Piccagliani.

A costumed pose. Callas in *Poliuto,* original Donizetti staging, 1960. © Private Collection. Photo: André Tubeuf.
A listening pose. Callas recording in London for Walter Legge.
© Private Collection. Photo: André Tubeuf.

Callas and Victor De Sabata at La Scala, 1954. It was under De Sabata's baton that Callas earned her first triumph at La Scala, in *Macbeth* (1952).
© Archivio Fotografico Teatro alla Scala. Photo: Erio Piccagliani.
Callas walks out on a performance of *La Sonnambula* to play the night-owl at Elsa Maxwell's costume ball in Venice, 1957. © Archive Photos.

77

Final Act of *La Traviata*. Violetta, dying of tuberculosis, bids farewell to Alfredo. Callas singing *Addio del passato*, the most heart-rending aria in this famous opera. The character's death earns immortality for the performer. © Sygma. Photo: D. Goldberg.

Callas being fitted by her favorite couturière, Madame Biki, in Milan (1958). Her hands and feet are gracefully posed. For what role? In what drama? © Sipa Press.
Make-up session. © Sygma.

Callas as La Sonnambula, directed by Luchino Visconti. La Scala, 1955. © Archivio Fotografico Teatro alla Scala. Photo: Erio Piccagliani.
For the ball in *La Traviata*, Callas was dressed in glittering mourning for a happiness that is no more. The gown was designed by Lila de Nobili, the performance directed by Visconti. Here, in 1956, is the supreme consummation of Callas's magic. © Archivio Fotografico Teatro alla Scala. Photo: Erio Piccagliani.

Callas in *Medea,* directed by Visconti. In 1969, Pier Paolo Pasolini made a film version of the Cherubini opera, also starring Maria Callas. © All rights reserved.
Last *Medea* season at La Scala, December 1961. Maria Callas turns her back on the footlights' glare to face the paparazzi's blinding flashbulbs. © Sygma.

Two opera stars and their husbands. Maria Callas with Battista Meneghini and Elisabeth Schwarzkopf with Walter Legge (who for ten years served as music director for Callas's recordings) dining at Biffi Scala in August 1954. © Private Collection. Photo: André Tubeuf.

The August 1954 gala at the Elysée Palace for Callas, now the darling of Parisian high society. © Archive Photos.
Maria Callas and Aristotle Onassis with dancers Margot Fonteyn and Rudolf Nureyev in Monte Carlo, August 1963. © Archive Photos.

Time off. Callas and Churchill deep in conversation on the deck of the *Christina*, anchored off Monaco, August 1959. © Archive Photos.

Maria and Ari, one of the most publicized couples of their time. Left: © Sygma. Right: © S.B.M.

Philadelphia, January 1959. American audiences are entranced by the soprano's physical presence. © Magnum Photos: René Burri.
Callas surrounded by a sea of fans at the stage-door of La Scala, following the May 1958 performance of *Il Pirata.* © Sipa Press.

Violetta the courtesan, cast down by the money Alfredo hurls into her face. *La Traviata* at La Scala, 1955. © Private Collection. Photo: André Tubeuf.

Farewell appearance in Paris, December 8, 1973. Elegant gown, piano accompaniment, a hail of bouquets, applause: a fitting farewell for the diva. © Sygma.

Admirers reaching out to touch their idol during her Paris farewell appearance, a charity gala at the Théâtre des Champs-Elysées in December 1973. A scene repeated less than a year later at Sapporo in Japan. © Archive Photos.

Heavy security surrounds Maria Callas as she arrives at the Paris Gare de Lyon railway station in December 1958. The diva made her Paris debut a few days later at a gala performance staged by the Paris Opéra. © Archive Photos

Prison of solitude. Callas, shown at home in 1963, already a phantom of the opera. © *Paris-Match*. Photo: Garofalo.
Prison of pleasure. Festive candlelight playing on the diva's face, 1958. © *Paris-Match*. Photo: Garofalo.

The editor would like to thank Alain Coblence, Andrea Vitalini (Théâtre de la Scala, Milan) and Colette Piron (Maria Callas Exhibition, Hôtel de Ville de Paris), as well as Colette (Paris-Match), Martine Detier (Sipa Press), Françoise (Associated Press), Thierry Freiberg (Sygma), Marie-Christine (Magnum), La Société des Bains de Mer, and Catherine Terk (Archive Photos).